THE ACTOR'S GUIDE TO BEING (ALMOST) FAMOUS

A Resource Book

Megan Ford-Miller

Copyright © 2020 Megan Ford-Miller

All rights reserved

No part of this book may be reproduced, or stored in a retrieval system, or transmitted in any form or by any means, electronic, mechanical, photocopying, recording, or otherwise, without express written permission of the publisher.

ISBN: 9798577064655

Cover design by: Megan Ford-Miller
Library of Congress Control Number: 9895917561
Printed in the United States of America

CONTENTS

Title Page	1
Copyright	2
Self-Tapes The New Audition	7
Live Virtual/Remote Auditions	13
Agent and Manager Etiquette	16
Actor Agent Commission Obligation	22
Performing Arts Expenses	25
Professional Performer Auto Expenses	28
The New Normal	30
Qualities Of A Professional Actor/Actress	32
Industry Terms	36
Coming Soon	67
About The Author	69
Praise For Author	71

Dear Actor/Actress/Mom/Dad/Friend/Supporter,

Everyone has a place in this industry if they have passion and drive and of love of the craft, they just have to stick with it long enough to figure out where exactly that is.

This is just one part of the information you will need on your journey. The most valuable part being the experience you will gain. But as you go along knowing the lingo and having the extra tools necessary to get started puts you a step ahead, especially after COVID-19 . Things move faster, the process has changed, and you need to know your rights as an actor/actress while working on a set as well.

Surrounding yourself with people who want to help you on this journey is very important. Find other people who have the same interests and support them, and you will hopefully get the same in return. You need a support system to survive long term in this industry because success does not happen quickly.

You will find an exhaustive industry terms resource along with tips, the current plan from SAG-AFTRA stating how we move forward and function with Covid-19. Also, tips, tools, and a little advice.

Break a leg I'm rooting for you!

Megan

SELF-TAPES THE NEW AUDITION

An actor will audition many more times in their career than they will actually work on a contracted job. For the most part it is a huge part of your career as an actor to get good at auditioning and that means self-tapes especially now in a post Covid-19 world more than ever.

You have heard the old expression "You only have one chance to make a good first impression." This is more than true in the acting world. It needs to be more than just a good impression it needs to be great.

The most common question I hear from people is "Do you think they really watch all of them?" *Them* being the tapes actors send in.

The answer? Yes.

This was already becoming the the standard for most casting directors. Now given the pandemic it is a way of life for casting going forward. Just like any audition it is weeding out process to get to an in-person audition. I heard a lot of people pre-covid-19 saying things like, "Industry is just being lazy." But it actually is just the reality of our world, everything is about video; we are in a visual era. They can see more people this way, and if they like it, they can watch it multiple times and send to the appropriate people faster.

GET TECHY or PAY SOMEONE!

Be creative find out who around you are good with video technology. Ask around and get referrals from other actors, agents, managers. But *do not* send in bad tapes, or bug your agent or manager about how to do it, they don't have time for it and it's your responsibility. It's part of the JOB of being an actor.

Odds are if you are a parent your child knows how to edit a video and send it. READ THE DIRECTIONS! Which they may not pay as much attention to, but you can handle that part.

Do not read the narrative only the lines of the characters, yes, new actors really do this!

Here is an example of an audition request read every line carefully it's all valuable information:

APPOINTMENT INFORMATION

Client: Your Name Here
Status: Self-tape, Called out, Audition, Call-back, Directors session etc.

Due: Sun, Apr 26, 2020   9:00 PM PDT
Role: John

13-16yo, Male. Open ethnicity. RECURRING Co Star
Material: Attached (Audition sides are included in this email)

Read For: Self-Tape

Meet With: Casting Director
Notes: **Pay special attention to Notes this comes directly from casting

Hi -
We would like your client to self-tape for the role of John in WEIRDER THINGS. Dates are TBD right now - please let us know if your client has any conflicts/commitments or is attached to anything this year.

PLEASE DO NOT POST THIS CONFIDENTIAL MATERIAL ON YOUTUBE, PUBLIC VIDEO SITES, OR ANY FORM OF SOCIAL MEDIA. We will not accept any submissions through VIMEO (or similar platforms), and any videos found on Vimeo (or similar platforms) will be reported to Netflix and must be removed immediately.

SCRIPT: Not available.

GENERAL NOTES:
- NO MAKEUP
- HAIR: Please wear hair pulled back away from the face in a low pony tail (for short hair - back in barrettes)
- Wardrobe: A plain t-shirt works great!

****SELF-TAPE INSTRUCTIONS:** Please upload audition clips to ECO-CAST.****

LABELING - Please label clips with your client's name and the character name.
Example:
John Doe.John.S1
John Doe.John.S2
John Doe - Slate

SLATE - SLATE IS MANDATORY.

Slate MUST INCLUDE:
- FULL NAME
- HEIGHT - AGE (if under 18)
- HOMEBASE (location)

- Full body shot

PLEASE UPLOAD THE SCENE AND SLATE AS INDIVIDUAL CLIPS!
Manager: Your manager's name or blank if you don't have one
Other Rep.: Agent – your agent's name if you have one

PROJECT INFORMATION
Project: WEIRDER THINGS
Type: Episodic
Start Date: approx. May
Wrap Date: Nov 2020
Location: Albuquerque
Union: SAG/AFTRA
Writer: John Doe
Network: Netflix, ABC, AMAZON, CBS, HBO MAX, ECT.
Casting Director: Look them up, what other projects have they casted?
Executive Producer: Producers will be listed I suggest you look them up and see their other work.
Cast: If there are well known actors already attached to the project they will be listed here.

Attachments area- Here you will find audition sides**

All of the information on this request is important to help you be as prepared as you can be for the audition. Including looking up the names of the producers and casting professionals to see their previous work. Who are the other actors attached? Are you supposed to be related in the script? What tone is the writer and directors previous work? There are clues here to help you do a great tape you just have to take the time to look.

WRONG   RIGHT

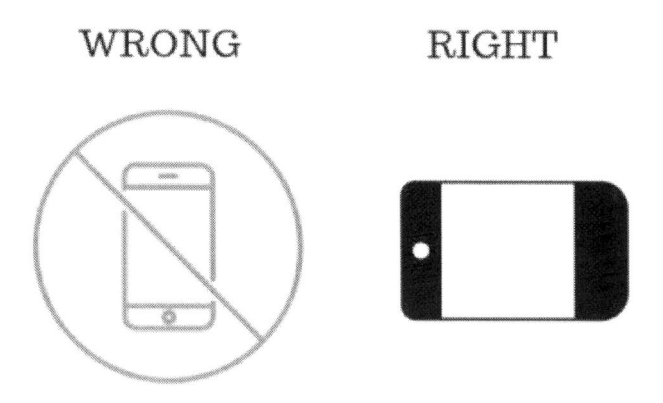

In the beginning keep it simple. A space in your house with good lighting I highly recommend investing in a standing ring light. Make sure it is a quiet space, a simple solid background or a blank wall is perfect. Even a sheet can work, I like a large piece of felt like material, so it doesn't wrinkle easily. If you have the luxury of painting a dedicated wall a light gray/blue is great for all skin tones. In addition a large cheap piece of plywood painted the perfect color can be great as well. Recording on your phone is fine if used right and always use a tripod.

Have a good reader, a reader's job is not to act it is only to read. When starting out the tendency is to think the person an actor is reading with has to also be acting but that is not the case. A reader should speak quietly and yes, they should understand the context of what is happening in the scene but not perform as an actor. The person auditioning should be front and center and be the only focus of the tape, overacting by a reader is not only a huge distraction but a huge pet peeve of casting directors.

Don't wait until the last minute and create a pressure cooker situation.

Make sure the files are small enough for easy upload and download I suggest filming scenes individually if there are multiple and labeling them Name/Role/SC1/TK1 or SC2/TK2, Slate etc.

And COACH! COACH! COACH!

I know, it all costs money but if you have one opportunity to make an impression investing in yourself and doing the best job is really what you should do.

> *"Look, if you had one shot, or one opportunity to seize everything, you ever wanted in one moment. Would you capture it or just let it slip?"*
> *—Eminem*

LIVE VIRTUAL/ REMOTE AUDITIONS

Whether doing a eco-cast live audition through Actors Access or a zoom audition just like for a self-tape be sure to have lighting, sound, and a background that is not a distraction.

Unlike with a self-tape you will have only one shot at getting it right, so I highly suggest practicing in advance to make sure everything works correctly.

If you are doing an eco-cast live, you will log in with the invitation sent to your Actors Access account and wait in a virtual waiting room. You will get a warning that lets you know you are "on deck" meaning your audition can start at any second. Similarly, with a zoom invite you will log in and wait for the other party to start the meeting.

Here are some things to do to help ensure things go smoothly:

- ✓ **Be sure you are on a dedicated network**
- ✓ **Disable notifications and turn on do not disturb**
- ✓ **Quiet space with a neutral background**
- ✓ **Good natural lighting, a ring light or similar**
- ✓ **Disable firewalls or pop-up blockers**

Just like a self- tape if your using a mobile device be sure it's turned to landscape position.

And be sure your computer/ mobile device are positioned at eye level and framed from mid-chest to top of your head.

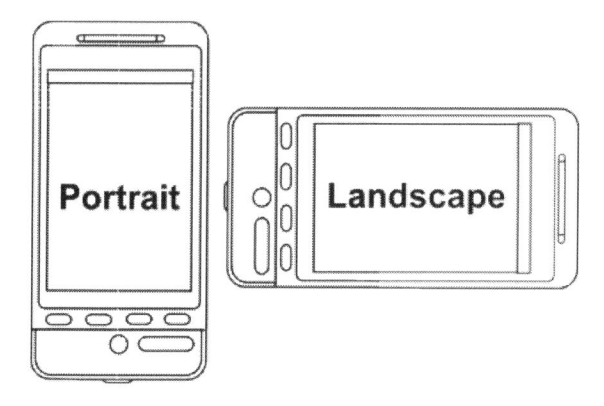

When doing a live audition on zoom you will most likely need to provide a reader, unlike eco-cast live which casting will have a reader for you. You may also be asked to tape the scenes seperately. Even though zoom can screen record the quality is not very good and that is why you may be asked to also tape the scenes, not the whole session just the scenes you audition with.

Specifically, for zoom remote live auditions and call backs you will need to create a basic ZOOM account if you do not already have one. Click e-vite link provided at appointed audition time. You will be held in a "waiting room" until all attendees are present on our end and joined by the host when everyone is ready.

REGARDING ZOOM SETTINGS:

-Please make sure both AUDIO and VIDEO settings are turned **ON**

-Please make sure you are in **GALLERY VIEW** once joined. You can find this setting option (small box icon) in the top right corner of your screen.

During the audition or call-back, you will be able to see yourself while reading which can be distracting for some. It is recommended to place a piece of paper or a book in front of the screen so you can focus on looking into the computer's camera.

Please make sure the camera is <u>not blocked</u> if you choose to do this. You may be asked to record the audition scenes but not entire ZOOM session they don't want that only the scenes themselves.

Be sure to label your scenes just like a self-tape.

Sc.1 Tk 1, Sc.1 Tk 2 (and so on). Please make sure the link is downloadable.

> *"Ignore the naysayers. Really the only option is, head down and focus on the job." – Chris Pine*

AGENT AND MANAGER ETIQUETTE

Right off the bat you should know, agents and managers probably don't do everything you think they do, or maybe even what you think they should do.

Even a very personable manager or agent doesn't have time to filter down to you all of the information you really need for success in this industry they are relying on you to do your part, the research. There is a large information gap that takes time, research, and experience to fill.

Having a collaborative attitude is really important for you and your representation or *Team.* Most industry reps do not consider it their job to educate you about the industry you have chosen to be a part of, they consider that to be your job, which it absolutely is.

If you were going to be a nurse, doctor, or lawyer you would educate yourself either by taking classes or working with someone who is more knowledgeable and learning from them, right? This is no different.

Be selective when communicating with your reps, try to figure it out first there are a lot of resources online. Do you remember the old fable *The Boy Who Cried Wolf*? Apply that lesson when asking your reps questions. Yes, of course you can ask questions, but the problem is when clients also think their rep is, tech support, counseling services, MapQuest, and any other concierge type of informational support.

Hollywood Mom Blog is a great one for young actors and parents, also sagaftra.org, backstage.com, castingnetworks.com, info.castingabout.com. I also recommend following casting directors on Facebook and Instagram. 2020 has created the opportunity for many of them to take to their social media platforms and talk to you directly with great advice for auditioning, you can look up casting directors here:

castingdirectorslist.com

NEVER bypass your agent or manger to get to a casting director or someone in production. If your reps don't trust you, they don't want you around. You are a TEAM, and it is in their best interest for you to succeed. When the stakes are high it's easy to become inpatient but there has to be trust in order for the agent/manager/client relationship to work.

BE PATIENT TAKE A BREATH a huge part of this industry is waiting, and waiting, and more waiting it is a recurring theme in the process of doing your job as an actor.

Whether you have an agent or a manger or both will be different for everyone. Reid has always had had both but there were times I felt like in the beginning we could have done without a manager because I was doing so much for him myself. Regardless of how your team looks, be respectful of their time you are not their only client so be selective on how often you contact them for questions. This may sound silly to some perhaps, but this is a huge issue among newer actors and parents and when decisions have to be made by an agent or manager and who they keep on their roster this behavior can be a factor in whether you stay or go.

This may be foreign to you right now if you are not represented yet, but if you are **seeking representation** my suggestion is joining pro.imdb.com and reaching out to agents and managers you research on IMDb. Everyone listed on IMDb is rated by a system called Starmeter this system works as a rating system and the lower the Starmeter number the better the rating. As an example, popular actors are typically in the top 5,000 on IMDb where a new actor with little to no credits may have a rating in the hundred thousand to millions even. Here is an example of how to approach an agent or manger for the first time:

Hello John Agent,

My name is Jane Doe, and I am seeking representation. I have included a (meaning one, not multiple) headshot and a links to my IMDb (if you have one) and my website (if you have one) and also my Actors Access/Casting Networks profile page.

Thank you so much for your time and I look forward to hearing from you!

Sincerely,

Jane

(818) 555-5555

Short sweet and to the point, this is the preferred type of correspondence. If you have all your profiles up to date this make this a pretty simple process. Don't stop at one or two, send at least 20 to start and see what happens.

Do not reach back out unless they respond to you. If they don't respond odds are, they are not interested or have someone similar to you on their roster already and reaching back out is not going to change that.

I have had many conversations with agents and managers over the years. If they had a "wish list" of their perfect client, here's what it would look like.

For some reason, many actors and parents of young actors tend to behave like they are the ONLY client their agent or manager reps when it comes to response times. Most Agents and managers are juggling anywhere from 25 to 100 clients at once, and sometime more of it's a large agency and they have shared clients as well. I think many starting out in this industry are operating on a high level of anxious energy when it comes to their career. So when any business needs to be handled it is done so with a heightened sensitivity. That's a nice way of saying, yes, the stakes are high but don't act desperate it's not a good look on anyone. Everyone in the early to mid-stages of their career is in the same boat all waiting to have that moment when someone says you're a perfect fit. In the meantime, if you are doing all these things you should be, you are not only setting yourself up for a win, but you are also doing your part for a team win!

Agents and Managers are dealing with many schedules and clients in all phases of their career. Being prompt is a really big deal when things can change in a matter of minutes.

Always pay attention and respond to audition emails in a timely manner, and always hit the reply ALL button because this keeps everyone on the same page.

If you are not a person who regularly checks their email you will definitely need to make an adjustment in your habits. I recommend being able to get email notifications on your phone so you can be responsive. Answer the phone when your reps call, odds are if they are calling it's important and most likely it's time sensitive. Asking your reps right up front how they prefer to communicate is really important. Knowing already that they prefer being contacted through text, email, or phone calls will save everyone time and potential frustration.

Other wish list items are getting your self-tapes done by the deadline and preferably with time to spare in case adjustments need to be made. If you are unable to audition for a certain time period, please communicate with your reps and book yourself out for that time. Prioritizing your acting over other sports and hobbies is a hard choice but this is important because it lets your reps know how serious you are about your career. Also, something to think about is if you and or your child likes other activities over auditioning and taking acting classes you should think long and hard if this industry is for you because it is a huge investment of time and money.

When Reps ask for new materials like headshots, paperwork, trying a new class, please listen. There's a reason they are asking you to do these things, it means they see something that needs to be improved and in order to compete you should comply and promptly.

All of this being said, follow your instincts. Having representation, you trust is very important and obviously there are people in this business just like any other business that are out for themselves. But be careful not to let your own insecurities place blame or distrust on your reps when things aren't going your way. When choosing reps don't just sign with someone because you want an agent or manager, make sure it's a good fit personality wise and also that you guys are on the same page as far as a career plan.

It is industry standard to let a rep know you are leaving their roster BEFORE you start looking for another agent/or manager. And preferably at the end of your contract if one was in place. Most reps will not consider taking you on or even entertaining a conversation, until you have left your previous agency unless there are extenuating circumstances.

Loyalty in this industry means alot...

There can truly be a great synergy with the right people and remember they are on your team and you all support each other.

ACTOR AGENT COMMISSION OBLIGATION

When we first started our journey I had no idea how agents and managers worked. I was familiar with a commision system from my insurance marketing and sales background. But as far as really understanding who gets what and how much, I was clueless.
Variables from this chart may be non-union vs union since this is a SAG scale of commissions. Also you will find some managers will ask for 15% instead of 10% if you are new. They say it's because you are "in developement" I say, maybe keep looking for a different manager.
The industry standard is 10% for Agents and managers .

Residuals are paid directly to you in most cases so make a habbit of paying your reps quickly when they come in so you don't get in a situation where you owe them money. You only need to pay residuals to reps that you were with when you booked and did the job.

State of employment	Los Angeles, Chicago, Detroit, Atlanta, Washington DC, & Hawaii	New York and all other areas
Television and Theatrical	No commission at scale. For commission	Commission is payable on scale employment.

	to be payable, employment must be at least scale + 10%	
Commercials	Commission is payable on scale employment.	Commission is payable on scale employment.
Residuals **Made for Broadcast Television (includes episodic, M.O.W., and animation) On:** *Prime Time	Commission is payable on all prime-time reruns if employment contract was overscale (at least scale + 10%)	If original employment is at scale, commission is payable for first and second reruns. If original employment is overscale (at least scale + 10%), commissionable on every rerun
* Network non-prime time, syndication	Commission is payable only when employment contract provides for overscale residual payment.	If residual is at scale, commission is payable for first and second reruns. If residual is overscale, commissionable on every rerun.
*Foreign	Commission is payable only when employment contract provides for overscale residual payment.	Commission is payable only when employment contract provides for overscale residual payment.
*Theatrical exhibition	Commission is payable only when employment contract provides for overscale residual payment	Commissionable.
* Basic cable, supplemental markets (includes pay TV & videocassettes/DVDs)	Commission is payable only when employment contract provides for overscale residual payment.	Commissionable.

Made for Basic Cable (includes episodic, M.O.W., and animation) on:		
*Basic Cable *Primetime *Network non-primetime, syndication *Theatrical Exhibition	Commission is payable only when employment contract provides for overscale residual payment.	If residual is at scale, commission is payable for first and second reruns. If residual is overscale, commissionable on every rerun.
*Foreign	Commission is	Commission is payable only

	payable only when employment contract provides for overscale residual payment.	when employment contract provides for overscale residual payment.
* Supplemental markets (includes pay TV, video-cassettes/DVDs)	Commission is payable only when employment contract provides for overscale residual payment.	Commissionable.
Made for Theatrical (includes animation) on: *Free television * Basic cable *Supplemental markets (includes pay TV, videocassettes/DVDs)	Commission is payable only when employment contract provides for overscale residuals.	Commission is payable only when employment contract provides for overscale residuals.
Commercials: *Reuse	Original 21 months. Commission is payable at scale.	Original 21 months. Commission is payable at scale.
* Renegotiations	Only when employment contract provides for overscale payments and does not reduce payment below minimum scale; or guarantee acceptable to performer.	Only when employment contract provides for overscale payments and does not reduce payment below minimum scale; or guarantee acceptable to performer.

***No commissions shall be payable on the following, no matter where you live:

Travel expenses, living expenses, or per diems

Reimbursement for travel, mileage, wardrobe, special hairdresser, etc.

Penalty payments (i.e., late pay, meal period violation, forced call, rest period violations, etc.)

Please be advised that if you work under a SAG-approved special agreement, please contact your local guild office to determine rules of commission ability.

*** Information available at

https://www.sagaftra.org/

PERFORMING ARTS EXPENSES

Training to be an actor is very expensive and most will not see any return on those expenses for many years, yes, I said *many* years to come. But perhaps if you start from the very beginning of your career knowing what you can actually count as an expense and what you cannot, this could be helpful going forward financially.

Accompanist and Audition Expense

Advertising and Publicity (website, photos, resume, Showfax, IMDb, Actors Access)

Agents' Commissions and Managers Fees

Auto Expense (use Automobile Expenses worksheet) Worksheet

Coaching/Classes and Lessons (voice, dance, acting, etc., No Gym Memberships)
Equipment/Business Software (Description of purpose)

Gifts for Business (limited to $25 per recipient per year)

Internet and/or Streaming Services (business percentage only)

Make Up and Hair Care (only when working)

Office Supplies, Stationery & Postage

Rental of Studio Space and/or Equipment

Repairs and Maintenance (Equipment, Instruments, Warranty Contracts, etc.)

Research and Misc. Supplies (Sheet Music, Books, DVDs, Scripts, iTunes, Headphones)

Stage Manager Supplies (Kit, First Aid, Blacks, Tools, other SM's expenses)

Tax Preparation, Legal Fees, Professional Fees (business–related only)

Telephone (business-percentage only or 100% for 2nd Line)

Tickets for Research (theatre, film, concert, dance, Netflix, only for yourself)

Tips and Gratuities (backstage, dressers, stage door personnel, etc.)

Trade Publications (Backstage, Variety, Performer Cues, Call Sheet, etc.)

Travel Expenses (use Out of Town worksheet – out of town airfare, lodging, etc.)

Transportation/Transit Seeking Employment (Public Transit, Taxi, Livery, Shuttle

Union Dues & Initiation Fees (include AEA & SAG-AFTRA "working" dues)

Wardrobe and cleaning (costumes & specialized dancewear – No Streetwear)

Meals for Business - locally (receipts should indicate who, what, where, when & why)

Equipment Expense (Cost, Date of purchase, % of use for business)

PROFESSIONAL PERFORMER AUTO EXPENSES

(MARRIED – Spouse Use Separate Form) NAME _____

If you operated a motor vehicle – one that you owned or leased – for Business, Charitable

Driving, Medical and Doctor Visits, please provide the following information.

If you are not sure what constitutes each of these categories, please discuss with a preparer

before completing this form.

YOU MUST COMPLETE THE STARRED * ITEMS

NUMBERS MUST BE ACTUAL – DO NOT ESTIMATE

*Year, Make and Model of Car _____

*Date Placed in Service _____

(Date you started using it for business?)

*TOTAL MILES DRIVEN _____ Miles

(Total miles from January 1 through December 31)

*COMMUTING MILES _____ Miles

(Driving to and from work)

*BUSINESS MILES _____ Miles

(Looking for work locally or out of town, Working out of town overnight, Driving

between two jobs on the same day, Going to a Class or Course, Doing Research)

CHARITABLE MILES _____Miles

MEDICAL MILES _____Miles

OTHER (Personal) _____Miles

Parking and Tolls

Business Parking & Tolls $_____

Medical Parking & Tolls $_____

Charitable Parking & Tolls $_____

THE NEW NORMAL

Not only should you as a professional actor/actress know the current safety protocols for being on a film/TV/commercial set or photo shoot, but in addition you need to know your rights to be protected and safe on that set as well. Be wary of productions that don't have your best interests in mind if they aren't willing to keep you safe it's not worth it.

Productions now are required to carry Covid-19 Insurance which is cost prohibitive and this has much to do with more limited productions working. Actors who book jobs will be required to Covid test on average 3 times week with one of those tests being a nasel swab. Craft services will only be able to provide boxed lunches so the actors "in it for the crafty" will most likely find this disappointing. Of coarse 6ft distancing and changes to fight scenes, and intimacy scenes are a given. This is an extremely resilliant industry full of creatives and I know it will come back in full force, but for now we have to make adjustments.

'The Safe Way Forward' is a Joint Report from the DGA, SAG-AFTRA, IATSE, and Teamsters on COVID-19 Safety Guidelines to Provide Safe Workplaces in a Pre-Vaccine World.

To find the entire document Google:
 The Safe Way Forward Sag-Aftra

Though non-union sets are not held to SAG-AFTRA standards they should be striving to meet them.

Also, go read White Paper which is the Alliance of Motion Picture and Television Producers safety committee task force plan which includes non-union productions.

To find the entire document Google:
Filmla Task Force White Paper

**These are the most current plans as of June 2020 and are subject to change and be updated.

QUALITIES OF A PROFESSIONAL ACTOR/ACTRESS

Being a professional is being a professional in any business. But different industries have specific areas that are stressed more than others. Like for example discretion, this is why every audition you receive comes with a warning about not sharing or posting the information. Actors have a tendency to want to shout to the rooftops when they get an audition especially if it's a significant project. I hate to say there have been many actors that have not gotten a job because they couldn't use discretion. Yes, it's exciting but it's also privileged information. It's details of someone's hard work that is not ready to be shared with the world, and they don't appreciate it when you do.

Discretion moves beyond auditioning and into actually booking a job and the behaviors you exhibit on a set. Whether it's taking photos on a set or giving other actors their own privacy being discreet is a tool that if you don't have it you need to work to develop it. This goes for parents of an actor or actress as well. Some of the worst sets I've ever been on had nothing to do with the crew which 99 percent of the time were professional, it was the parents. Some of them chomping at the bit to ask you a million questions and compare agents, managers, and resumes. Don't be that person, the crew doesn't appreciate it either and you will quickly become THAT person that everyone avoids. That being said we have made lifelong friends on sets, when you are genuinely doing your best to create a positive environment for artists to work you will have an amazing experience. If you try to compare yourself to everyone around, you and make it a competition it will be miserable for everyone.

As an actor/actress if you can't arrive on time to an audition or a set, you're in trouble. Sometimes casting gets behind and people have to wait a long time I get it, but you still need to arrive on time to an audition. And if you are late to a set you are literally costing them money so start the good habit of being on time now and make it priority. If you are consistently late to a set you won't be asked back if they have that option and if not, you may get a phone call from a producer, either is not good for your reputation.

Here is a list of qualities you can strive for that will make you not only a professional but a better client and a sought-after actor.

Hard Worker- Despite what anyone says being an actor is a job and it's hard work

Committed- Acting is a long-term career commitment and success takes time. In order to be successful your acting has to be the priority which may mean putting it above social opportun-

ities and making hard choices.

Intelligent- Actors are very intelligent people who don't just memorize lines but understand how human beings behave and find those qualities in themselves.

Being Punctual- Whether it's an audition or a meeting you understand people's time is valuable and you want to make a good impression. If it's a set, you understand that it runs on a schedule and time = money.

Being Discreet- You may have access to privileged information for an audition or on location to work. Treating a set like a workplace should be the mindset and always keeping information to yourself unless you've been given permission to share it.

Empathy- A good actor must be able to be vulnerable and be in touch with their own feelings and care about others.

Kindness- always be kind as an actor if you have some success like it or not you will be judged more harshly than someone else.

Energy and stamina- Actors have to do the same over and over until it's right and also work long hours, standing for long periods of time. Some people may try to say acting is not a job, it most certainly is.

Patience & Self-Control- Waiting is really hard and an actor will need to be able to refrain from excessive calls, and emails to managers and agents, even production. Yes, call sheets typically don't go out until the night before a shoot and sometimes only 12 hours before because they are sent at wrap if it's already in production.

Driven- Always learning and wanting to get better and taking classes

Resilience- Being told no is difficult and an actor is told that hundreds and hundreds of times. They have to be able to re-focus and move forward to the next opportunity.

Highly Imaginative- As an actor you have to think outside the box and try to make choices in your acting that maybe someone else wouldn't it takes creativity to stand out in a very competitive field.

Not Compare yourself to others- This is the biggest and most common mistake actors make and it's very difficult not to do it. You are you; they are them, and your journey is not their journey. No two people are alike, and job can be lost or booked over something as trivial as blue eyes or brown eyes. Just don't do it! It is detrimental to your self-esteem and not helpful for you in the long term.

INDUSTRY TERMS

10-1: A term used instead of saying someone from the cast or crew is in the bathroom, they are "10-1"

18TPY: Eighteen to play younger is exactly as it sounds. Someone over the legal age of 18 to play a character who is a minor.

1st AD: The 1st AD is the person that creates the shooting schedule and manages the crew during the film production. Also, they are typically the person calling out commands to the crew and initiating the shoot itself (sound! camera! action!)

1st and 2nd Asst Camera: Exactly what it sounds like, they assist the DP or Cinematographer.

Abby Singer: Is the second to last shot on a film set. It is the shot right before the martini. Named after a Hollywood Producer. He let his crew know two shot out before they had to start wrapping the set.

Act: To Perform.

Actor: A trained professional who acts/performs on stage, or in film, or television.

Act: Feature film scripts are split into Three Acts – Act I, Act II, Act III. Each act contains the major plot points and scenes that make up the script.

Action: The call to start a scene when filming usually said by the 1st AD or Director.

Action: In a script is the movement in scene that pushes the story forward. What's happening on screen.

Adapt/Adaptation: a screenplay based on pre-existing source material (Includes short stories, plays, articles, novels, comics/graphic novels, video games, etc.).

Adjustment: Something given to actors by a casting director during an audition, or a director while filming.

Ad Lib: When an actor improvises dialogue in a scene.

ADR-Looping- Automated dialogue replacement, also called looping. During the editing process the actor is called to a sound studio where he/she's scene is played back so they can rerecord the lines, often because of outside sound.

Agency: An organization that secures work for talent in the entertainment business; essentially an employment agency for actors and entertainers.

Agent: a person who finds jobs for actors, authors, film directors, musicians, models, producers, professional athletes, writers, and other people in various entertainment businesses. They make 10% of earning from client bookings.

Ambiguous: This is referring to an actor who is of mixed ethnicity.

Antagonist: The villain which can be a person, society, nature, etc.

Arbitration: When there is a dispute regarding credits or pay a third party will be brought in to arbitrate between parties.

Art Dept.: The art department of a film or tv show is made up of a Production Designer any or some of the following: Art Director, Art Dept. Coordinator, Carpenters, Scenic Artists, Buyer, Set decorator, Set Dresser, Art PA's. This is a typically a large part of the crew as they are creating the world the story is told in.

Attached (or Attachment): Commitment by talent (actor) to being in your film. Often used for pitching and gathering funding.

Audition: A scene performed in front of a casting director, director, or producers to obtain a role in a production.

Background (or b.g.): Actors moving behind the main action usually non-speaking.

Backstory: Your characters' background. Often not seen in the film but good for building your character.

Back to one: If you think of your beginning position in a scene as one, that's where you need to return when they call cut and start the scene again.

Banana: When walking through a scene you will do a slight curve rather than a straight path, like a banana. You can do a right banana or a left banana.

Basecamp: Where the makeup, costume, and cast trailers are located, as well as crew parking and catering. It's you will report to when arriving for work.

Beat: A plot point.

Beat Sheet: A list of all the scenes in the movie in the order they appear.

Beauty Shot: The final scene of a television show used for the credits.

Best Boy: The best boy is a term used for the person of either gender who is the foreman under the key grip or gaffer. This position often works as a "swing" for both departments.

Bible: (TV Show Bible): When creating an original TV series, this document contains all the information related to the show including concept, setting, characters, their bios, and their interactions with one another, and sample episodes in logline plus one paragraph synopsis format.

Big eyes: When the A.C. (assistant cameraman) is focusing for a close-up, he/she will usually ask the actor for "big eyes" and you want to provide exactly that, without blinking or looking away, until focus is set.

Billing: In what order and actors name is placed in the credits. There can be front billing at the beginning more often with TV. Or end credit billing.

Bio: Short for Biography. A description of the actors background. On IMDb there is a section for a short and a long bio.

Bit Part: A role in which there is direct interaction with the principal actors, but no more than five lines of dialogue.

Blocking: When filming the director will invite actors to set before there scene to work out or rehearse the scene.
Blue Screen: When Special effects need to be added actors often work in front of a large blue screen. The effects are added in post-production.

Body Double: Being a body double is the job of people who take the place of performers during the filming of a scene for a television or motion picture production. A body double doesn't have to have facial resemblance to the performer. But overall skin tone, body type, height, and color of hair are often considered essential in order to achieve the proper effect. Often, the double is filmed from the back or at a distance.

Bookends: Scene at the (1) beginning of the movie, defining the setting and plot and (2) at the end of the movie, wrapping everything up.

Booking: When an actor is hired to play a role in a production.

Boom Operator: Part of the sound team in a film crew that operates the boom mic. Must hold their arms up for long periods of time and sometimes get into awkward positions to get the sound.

B-Story: Major subplot. Usually carries the theme, the subconscious goal, the secondary characters.

Break a Leg: A sentiment of "good luck" to actors.

Breakdown: These are the casting notices that agent's and manager's work from to attach submit their clients for roles. They are descriptions of the project and the characters casting is looking for.

Breaking Character: Sometimes an actor will become distracted and break their character or be pulled out of the scene.

Bump: This refers to an actor receiving a "bump" in pay for doing work that requires them to be uncomfortable or is riskier.

Buy Out: Sometimes it is better for a production company to negotiate a weekly rate or buy out instead of paying the day rate. This is common with Guest-Star roles then they have you available for the week no matter your workdays if things need to be moved around in the schedule.

C47: Simply a clothespin. Very versatile for set use and used on film sets a lot. Some say it was named after the C-47 airplane because of its versatility.

Call Back: When actor is called back to meet with casting again after the initial audition.

Call Sheet: The document sent out in advance with the crew and cast call times and schedule for that shooting day.

Call Time: A time specifically for you to arrive to set, it may be different than anyone else's.

Camera Crew: The camera team.

Camera left-right: This is from the perspective of the camera. If you're facing the camera, camera left will be your right.

Camera Ready: Sometimes you may be asked to arrive "camera Ready" This means you have done your own hair and make-up and are wearing what you will wear on camera.

Casting: The process of auditioning and hiring actors.

Casting Call: AKA open call this is a casting open to anyone who fits the criteria.

Casting Director: The casting director is hired by a project whether film, tv, commercial, print, music video. When casting a production, which includes working closely with the director while auditioning, and negotiating rates of pay for the actors hired.

Casting Notice: Casting notices are like breakdowns but available to the public.

CHSPE: The California High School Proficiency Exam. You must be 16 years old or in the second semester of your sophomore studies to take the exam.

Champagne Roll: at 100 film rolls, or in more modern terms 100 hard-drive downloads on a digital shoot, into a shoot, the cast and crew get a celebratory glass of champagne.

Changes: This a wardrobe term that refers to an actors clothing changes throughout a shoot.

Character: The people the story is about.

Character Arc (or Arc): The path of your character's transformation across the entire story.

Cheat toward the camera: When you are having a conversation with someone, you naturally face him. Sometimes when filming or auditioning, we'll ask you to slightly turn more toward the camera so that we can see your expressions—hence "cheating" toward the camera.

Cinematographer or Director of Photography: This position is the over the camera and light crews working on a film, television production or other live action piece and is responsible for making artistic and technical decisions related to the image.

Clapper: Is another name for the slate. It will have a place to write the scene, take, and shot. Also, the production title, director, and director of photography or cinematographer. When you hear the "clap" sound an "action" will follow.

Climax: The highest point of the drama in the script. Happens in Act III usually before the resolution.

Close up: When the camera is focused solely on one performer in a close frame.

Clunky: Refers to awkward dialogue.

Cold Read: When an actor is asked to read sides (materials) that they have not had time to prepare or work on.

Color Cover: A professional who stands in for an actor wearing the same color.

Commission: Actors pay a ten percent commission to their agent and or manager of their pay for a job.

Company Move: When filming and the whole film crew moves to a new location to start a new scene.

Comp Card: AKA a composite. This is a card with several pictures of an actor or model showing several different looks.

Copy: Another term for a script for TV, radio, commercial, and voice over.

Complication: An obstacle.

Conflict: When characters goals oppose one another.

Copy That: Means yes, I understand. It also lets the person know you received the information as it is really important for things to run efficiently on a set.

Co-Stars: Co-stars generally have only one or two lines or one or two scenes. While it's not guaranteed, you will likely only work one day.

Costume Designer: A costume designer is a person who designs costumes or the wardrobe for a film, stage production or television. They are the head of that dept and under them are usually an assistant or two and shoppers, possibly a seamstress as well.

Cover shot: An additional angle of the master shot for editing purposes in filming.

Craft Services: On set catering.

Crane Shot: A shot taken with camera on a crane from above. It's a saying in the industry that it's not a blockbuster unless there is a crane shot.

Crawl: A term that refers to the ending credits.

Credit: A person's name and title or character name in a resume, IMDb, or film/television show credits.

Crew: Everyone involved in the productions with the exception of the actors.

Crew Call: This is when the film crew usually everyone besides actors starts their workday. Be sure as an actor to check your individual call time.

Crisis: Hero faces deepest fears to overcome the antagonist and innermost fears.

Cue: This is a signal given to an actor letting them know when to take action.

Cut: This is the end of the scene called out by the director or 1st AD letting actors know they can break character and the camera stops rolling.

Cutaway: This is when a continuous scene cuts to another shot and then cuts back to the first shot.

Dailies: Raw footage of the previous day of filming to be reviewed.
Day Player - A principal performer hired daily, rather than a long-term contract.

Dead Cat: Is that fuzzy cover that goes over a boom mic to block wind and distortion.

Deal Memo: Written follow-up to a verbal agreement an actor will receive this before an actual contract.

Demo Reel: A video compiled of clips from on screen performances showcasing an actor's skills. AKA a showreel.

Development: Process of script revisions with the production company or studio.

Dialogue: What the characters say.

Dilemma: Problem for your hero. A choice between two very difficult choices.

Director: The director is responsible for overseeing all aspects of the film or TV show being created. They control the artistic direction and are involved in all aspects of the production.

Dolly: Refers to a camera move and also the equipment that moves the camera.

Dolly Grip: the person on the crew who is in charge of working with this piece of equipment.
Double: A professional used in place of a principle actor, different than a stand-in.

Dramady: A drama and a comedy in one.

Dramatic Action: What compels your protagonist to keep moving forward as they are trying to solve a problem.

Dressing Room: A space that is the actors to change or just have their own space during filming. This can be required contractually for union actors.

Elevator Pitch: When you pitch your yourself to someone in about 30 seconds.

Ensemble: In film this implies everyone's role is more equal and there are no real principle characters.

Established: When a person or character has been filmed in a particular place or way, they have been established in the shot.

Entertainment Attorney: These types of attorneys can actually represent you to a production company, talent, director, or studio.

Ethnicity: Referring a person's race or ethnic makeup.
Entrance (Character Entrance): The first time we see a new character in the script.

Exit: This can refer to an actor leaving a scene. It can also be used as "Actor John Smith has exited the series."

EXT.: In a script this refers to an exterior scene.

Extra: Another term for a background actor typically a non-speaking role.

Exposition: Background information of your

story and characters.

Feature Film: A modern feature can be anywhere from 80 minutes to 180 minutes.

Featured: This is referring to a role that may have a line, or even one word but may be with a principle performer.

Field Rep: A representative of the SAG-AFTRA union that visits sets and make sure actors are well and standards are being upheld.

First Look Deal: When a production company has to take all their projects to a particular studio.

First Team: This refers to the principle actors on a production.

Five Percenter: A term used when referring to an actor's legal representation who is paid 5% of their earnings.

Flashback: In script when we cut back to a scene in the past in the story.

Forced Call: When cast and crew have to report back to set within 12 hours of wrapping the previous day.

Four-banger: A large trailer with four dressing rooms. There are also double- and triple-bangers and so on.

Fourth Wall (as in "Breaking the Fourth Wall"): A stage play term. The invisible wall between the audience and the actors. If broken, means that the character is showing his/her awareness of the audience and speaking directly to them.

Gaffer: The gaffer is the chief electrician on a film or TV show. They are in charge of planning and executing the lighting scheme.

Genre: The category/type of film or script. Examples: Action/Adventure, Biographical (bio-pic), Character Drama, Comedy, Cutting Edge Independent, Drama, Epic, Drama, Family Animation (i.e. Pixar), Family, Live Action, Fantasy, Horror, TV (Comedy), TV (Drama), Musical, Period, Religious/Spiritual, Romantic Comedy, Science Fiction, Thriller/Crime Drama, War, and Western, horror, sci-fi, fantasy.

Greenlight: A Studio or production company is ready to produce a film.

Green Room: A holding space for actors not far from where they may be needed.

Green Screen: Similar to a blue screen used for the same purpose. Special effects, motion capture etc....

Grip: A grip is a position on a film crew whose main purpose is 'camera support'. If the camera needs to be on a dolly, then the grip department will manage the implementation of the dolly, or any other similar gear.

Groucho: When an actor needs to crouch a bit as he approaches the camera because the cameraman can't tilt up and still focus. You can also do a "reverse Groucho."

Guest Stars: Being a guest star generally means getting to work for a full week on a production typically getting billing at the beginning of the show and having a few, if not many, lines, and scenes.

Hack: term for a writer who is paid to write low-quality, rushed articles or books "to order", often with a short deadline.

Hand-Held: A popular style of filmmaking where the camera is not on a tripod. Used frequently in action and horror film genres.

Hand Props: Props an actor may hold to help tell the story.

Headshot: A photo of an actor printed out in 8x10 or 8.5x11 to take to auditions and industry meetings. Though many casting offices have gone green and it would just be available to view online.

Hero: Your protagonist. The character to which the story is being told from their perspective.

HMU: Hair and Make-up Department for a production.
Holding: A room where extras are held during production.

Honey Wagon: Not anything as appealing as the name. It is a truck trailer or combination of both with a number of dressing rooms for the actors. These either have individual toilets or a communal set built into the rear for cast and crew while on set.

High Concept: A concept that can be articulated in one sentence, easily marketable, and widely appealing.

Hook: What about the story pulls us in "What's
the hook?"

Hot Set: Meaning everything is placed for the scene do not move anything unless you are asked to move or use it in the scene and place it back in the same place after.

Improvisation: When acting coming up with a line or action without any previous preparation on the spot.

Inciting Incident: The one thing that happens
to your hero that forces them to take action and start the story journey.

Indie: Refers to Independent films that function the same way as a studio, just with a smaller budget.

Industry: The biz. Hollywood.

Intercut: When used, denotes that the action is moving back and forth between two or more scenes or when two are talking on the phone and appear on screen.

INT.: In a script refers to an interior scene.

Juicer: This is what film crew's call the set electrician.

Lead Actor/Actress - The main protagonist in the production. It is typically the largest role.

Legs & Sticks: On a set mean tripod. Watch where you're going there's typically a camera attached to them.

Lighting Designer: This is the crew member responsible for the productions lighting.

Locations Manager: Is the crew member responsible for finding and securing locations to be used. Obtains all fire, police, and other governmental permits. Also handles any logistical issues that may arise.

Location: This is the specific place where scenes for a production will be filmed.

Logline: 1-2 sentence description of a film or show.

Long Shot: When the camera framing includes the actors full body.

Lunch: The meal served halfway through a 12-hour shooting day. Union rules require lunch to be 6 hours from crew call you could have lunch at three in the morning depending on the call time for that day.

Manager: A Representative that manages your
career and helps find you work for a 10% commission.

Mark: An actors mark is where they have been told by the director to stand to get the best lighting and angle for the shot.

The Martini: The last shot of the day, meaning "the last shot is in the glass!"

Master Shot: This is a wide shot that establishes the principle actors and the background for that scene.

Matching Action: And actor must be able to remember to do the same action in each take of a scene.

Material: Refers to the script or audition sides. You will see "materials emailed" in an audition request.
Meal Penalty: Union actors will be paid extra when the production does not break in the proper window of time for breaks and lunch.

Meet Cute (or Meet-Cute): The moment in romantic comedies when the two potential romantic partners meet.

Mentor: Character in the script that helps the hero learn something about themselves. There are also False Mentors–characters who we think are allies, but are really enemies in disguise, working against the hero the whole time.

Midpoint: Usually right in the middle of the film. It's
where the protagonist experiences a false victory or defeat, must

fully commit to the story.

Monologue: a long speech for one character without breaks for dialogue with another character. Used for auditions mostly.

Montage: Like Series of short visuals used to show a series of related events.

MOS: Stands for motor only shot a scene is shot without sound.

M.O.W. (Movie of the Week): Television movie. AKA Made For TV Movie.

Multi-Camera: typically, a sitcom TV show also called multi-cam comedy.

Notes: Feedback from a casting director about your performance.

Obstacle: Anything that stands in the way of your hero achieving their goal.

Off Book: When an actor has their sides or lines memorized completely.

Off Camera: Dialogue that takes place off screen or camera.

Off Screen (O.S.): Denotes that we hear a character's dialogue, but they are not on camera.

On Book: When an actor is still rehearsing using their script or sides.

On The Nose: When deciding what to wear for an audition don't be too obvious or overly theatrical with, your choices.

Open Call: A general audition meaning anyone can audition.

Opening Credits: The production credits shown in the beginning of a film or TV show.

Out of Frame: When an actor is outside of the cameras framing.

Outline: A detailed breakdown of all the scenes in a script before it's written.

Over The Shoulder Shot: The camera focuses on one actor from over the shoulder of another actor.

Overtime: When a production works longer than the contractual day.

Pace: The rhythm of the script, fast paced, snappy dialogue.

Pan: This is a camera move it is sweeping shot from one side to the other.

Pantomime: this is when you pretend to be speaking conversationally. Background actors or extras will have to do this frequently to create atmosphere when filming.

Pass: Simply NO. "I will pass on this project."

Pay or play- When an actor, director, or writer gets paid whether the project is made. You either get paid or you'll be acting in the project.

Per Diem: Union projects require this to be paid when an actor is on location filming. It is a daily allowance for costs incurred while filming. Usually for food and laundry. They can be given as cash in an envelope or deposited in your bank account with your paycheck weekly.

Period Piece: Film or script set in a different time period.

Photo double - An actor who resembles a principal actor who is used to perform on camera in place of that person.

Pickup: Starting from a specific place in the scene that is not necessarily the beginning.

Pickup Shot: Sometimes in post-production the director or editor may find something missing or needed and have to go back and pick-up a scene after the fact.

Picture's Up: This is a warning shouted by many crew members letting everyone know the camera is rolling and the director is about to call "action!"

Pilot: This is the first episode of a TV series. Sometimes only a pilot is filmed and then used for pitching and getting funding for the whole series.

Plot: The sequence of events in your story. It's what happens from start to finish.

Plot Points: Moment in script that moves the plot forward and goes in a new direction.
Points: Monies accrued according to a pre-negotiated percentage in your contract if a certain profit is made in film or television.

Points (on-set): You will hear this yelled out a lot on set. It means move out of the pay and pay attention thing are being moved near you.

Point Of View (P.O.V.): Shot from the character's point of view.

Post-Production: This is the phase where filming is complete, and the editing process begins.

Poster: The actual poster for a film or television show.

Premise: The concept of a screenplay.

Pre-production: This is the preparation phase before filming actually begins. Casting, location scouting, hiring, design.

Principal Actor - A performer with lines.

Prodco: Production Company.

Producer: Person with most control on a film. He/she is responsible for every aspect of the film production process from start to finish. Including finding the material, securing fundraising, attaching talent, hiring key positions (Director, DP, Costume Designer, etc.), and arranging distribution. There are many types of producers because it is a big job. Examples are: Executive Producer, Producer, Co-Producer, Associate Producer, Assistant Producer, Production Director, Line Producer, Production Supervisor, and Administrative Producer.

Production Assistant (PA): This job can be specifically assigned to one particular aspect of a production like a talent PA, or just a general worker available to anything that needs to be done.

Profile: Side angle of the actor.

Project: The film or television show.

Prop Master: A prop master is the person who supervises the use of props, in a theatrical production or on a film. As an actor if you have props for a scene be sure they are safely returned to the prop master. If lost it can cause a continuity issue for the production.

Props: Or Properties are various objects which are used by actors and actresses during their scenes.

Protagonist: Main Character and the hero of the story.

Raise the Stakes: When you create a situation where the protagonist has more to lose. Obtaining his goal becomes riskier, both physically and emotionally.

Reader: the person who will read sides for an audition with you. They will read all of the other characters except the role you are auditioning for.

Recurring: The actor returns as the same character over multiple episodes, either on a standing contract or contracted periodically, with payment based on the terms negotiated and the number of appearances.

Red Herring: Element intended to distract the reader/viewer from a more important event in the plot.

Release: A legal document that must be signed before filming begins typically authorizing the use of your image.

Representation: Refers to someone who works on
your behalf to get you work or negotiate agreements. Usually refers to an agent or manager.

Reprise: When a character comes back to play the same role later.

Residuals: Payment made to the actor for subsequent showings, screenings, use of productions they have appeared in. If it was a union project and included in the contract.

Resume: An actors list of credits and special skills typically condensed to one page.

Reversal: An obstacle that sends the protagonist in the

opposite direction.

Rewrite: When a screenplay is edited or altered.

Rights: Legal permission to adapt source material for a screenplay.

Rings False: Something about a character and/or his/her dialogue does not seem accurate or consistent.

Rising Action: When the character has heightened emotional situations throughout the script.

Rolling!: A direction given for the camera to start recording.

Rom-Com: Romantic Comedy.

Room tone: The "silence" recorded at a location or space when no dialogue is spoken. Every location has a distinct presence. This is crucial for post-production sound mixing. You are meant to stand still and not make a sound.

Run & Gun: This filmmaking style is typically a very small crew and only a few pieces of equipment. Usually handheld.

Running Time: This is the length of any moving media film, tv, or commercial.

Rush Call: This is a last min booking of an actor or extras.

Scale: When a project hires you at scale, meaning the basic minimum amount they have to pay you according to SAG-AFTRA.

Scenario: A plot outline.

Screenplay By: Credit used to denote that you wrote the

screenplay.

Scribe: Another term for a screenwriter or TV writer.
Script: Material written for film or television.

Script Supervisor or Scripty: A script supervisor is a member of a film crew who oversees the continuity of the motion picture including wardrobe, props, set dressing, hair, make-up, and the actions of the actors during a scene. The notes recorded by the script supervisor during the shooting of a scene are used to help the editor cut the scene. They are also responsible for keeping track of the film production unit's daily progress.

Second Team: This refers to the stand-ins for the principle actors.

Segue: The transition from one shot to the next.

Selections: This term refers to the wardrobe selected for the actors.

Set: Any location where filming is taking place.

Set Designer: Crew member responsible for the set's design.

Set-Up: When the camera changes position in the same scene during filming.

Sequence: Series of related scenes connected by a particular problem or storyline.

Series of Shots: a director may ask for a series of shots. Meaning you will do the same scene several times trying it different ways.

Series Regular: The actor is under exclusive contract with the show to appear (or be paid regardless of appearing) every week.

Set Pieces: Part of the film or television set and actors are not to move things. See Hot Set

Shingle: Small enterprise/business, often set up by an actor or established player at a larger company.

Short: A short film. A short film is any film under 60 minutes in length.

Sides: The materiel from the project sent to an actor/actress to perform for their audition.

Single Camera: Usually refers to TV comedies using only one camera.
Shooting Script: The version of the script that includes scene numbers and camera direction.

Shop: When a script is passed around to producers and studios to be sold or optioned.

Short List: When you're being considered for a role, but the decision has not been made yet. Usually when a production in a very early stage.

Showrunner: The person running a TV show managing the day-to-day operations, hiring, and firing, etc. Oftentimes it is the writer/creator of the show.

Sitcom: Situation comedy on TV.

Slate: List of films scheduled for production.

Slate: (AKA Clap Slate in filming) the main purpose is to tell the post-production team when the camera has started (and stopped) recording.

Slate: An actor will slate in the beginning of an audition stating name, age (if under 18), location. The information asked can vary sometimes height or a full body shot.

Slip: As in "slipped your script." A representative secretly forwards someone a script before anyone else gets to review and/or consider it, or as an unofficial
submission for co-production, casting, rewrites, etc. Always a secret.
Slug or Slug line: When reading a scene in a screenplay it describes location and time of day.
Example- INT. OFFICE – DAY

Soliloquy: A monologue that speaks to the inner thoughts or perspective of that character.

Sound Mixer: In film the sound mixer is responsible for all of the sound recording on location or in a studio and is considered the head of the sound department. The sound mixer is in charge of hiring/supervising the boom operator and utility sound technician for the project.

Source Material: Any original material adapted for the screen.

Spec Script: A spec is written for a project with no intention of selling it is to written or filmed showcase talent in particular area mostly writing or directing.

Spine: The through line of your story, the main story.

Stage left-right: In theater, stage left and right refer to the actor's left and right when facing the audience.

Stage-Mom: A parent of an actor who is very involved in the shaping of the acting career of the minor. Sometimes as a manager or in addition to a manager.

Stand-in: A background/extra performer who is used as a substitute for the principal actor for the purpose of setting up the upcoming shot. This allows the director of photography to set the lights and rehearse the movement that will take place in front of the camera.

Stepping on lines: When actor speaks his/her lines too early and talks at the same time or over the other actor.

Stinger: These are the bright orange extension cords and there will be many of them on a set. Don't ever plug anything in on a set without first asking, it could damage equipment and stop production.

Story Analyst: Usually a script reader at a studio.

Story By: This is a credit awarded to the author of an original screenplay.

Strike: To take down the set.

Striking: When lights are turned on the set.

Studio: A room or space where filming takes place.

Stunt: An action considered to be dangerous usually done by a stunt person.

Stunt Coordinator: A trained professional who coordinates stunts for a film or TV show.

Stunt Person - A specially trained performer who performs stunts on camera.

Submission: When an actor or his/her reps respond to a breakdown or casting notice with the actors information in hopes of getting an audition.

Subtext: The unwritten sentiment beyond the words an actor is saying.

Subplot: B-story of your script. Usually carries the theme, the subconscious goal, the secondary characters.

Subtext: The unstated, unspoken, oblique feelings the characters are having or implying.

Supporting Actor/Actress: A speaking role that is less than that of a lead actor, but larger than a bit part.

Synopsis: Condensed version of the screenplay plot usually one page.

SW: A call sheet term used next to an actors name to indicate they are starting work this day.

SWF: A call sheet term when next to an actors name indicates that they will start and finish their role in one day.

Swing: A crew position where someone is assisting both the Grip and Gaffer on a set.

Tagline: A phrase, slogan, or short sentence on the movie poster that represents the premise of a film.

Take: For writing, means your version, point of view, or even pitch on a particular concept or idea…as in "What's your take on this, screenwriter?"

Take 5: A five-minute break.

Talent: A term used for actors. The talent.

Teleplay: Script for a TV show.

Teleprompter: A machine that allows for an actor to look right into camera while saying their lines.

Ten-Percenter: A representative who takes 10% of your earnings this usually means an agent or manager.

Three Bells: On a sounds stage indicates filming has started.

Tight Shot: The camera focuses on one thing with little frame space. Tight framing.

Ticking Clock: Usually what happens at the midpoint of the script. Your hero is now under the gun to solve the problem before he runs out of time.

Tilt: A vertical camera move.

Timing: The perfect moment as an actor to do or say something.

Title: The name of a film or television show.

Topping: One actor delivering a more powerful line than the other actors previous.

Top Five: You may hear this term when someone is referring to the top 5 talent agencies. Traditionally these have been, WME (William Morris Agency), UTA (United Talent Agency), CAA (Creative Artists Agency), ICM (International Creative Management, and APA (Agency for the Performing Arts)

Tracking Shot: Camera filming on the move tracking a character.

Trades: Media outlets that focus on the entertainment industry.

Trailer: The commercial for a film it can vary in length and a studio can release several versions before a movie premier.

Transpo: The transportation dept. of a production that handles all the driving whether moving equipment or cast and crew.

Treatment: Short story version of a screenplay or teleplay. A detailed explanation more so than an outline.
Turnaround: When a studio develops a project, but decides not to move forward with it.

Twelve Point Courier: The standard and ONLY font used in screenplays. Variations: Final Draft Courier, Courier New.

Two-hander, Three-hander: A movie with two or three lead characters.

Two Shot: A shot with two actors in frame.

Under 5: You appear prominently in a scene but without lines, that it may be misleading if you have lines. This is an AFTRA contract term for a role with between one and five lines. You could also use the term "Featured," but it is so often applied to a role as an Extra or background actor.

Understudy: A performer hired to do a role only if the featured actor is unable to perform; used primarily in theatre.

Union: SAG-AFTRA is the actors union it is in place to protect performers rights, regulate pay, and hours.
Unsolicited: Sending your materials that has not been requested via official channels, to industry professionals.

Upgrade: When someone in production gets moved up to a better position.

VFX: Are visual effects for film, tv, or other media that can't be created during live action filming. Usually supervised by a visual effects supervisor on-set.

Voice Over (V.O.): When a character narrates a story as the character.

W: Call sheet term indicates an actor is working that day.

W/N: Call sheet term indicating an actor will be working that day, but the time has not been decided yet.

Waiver: The unions' approval to deviate from a contract.

Wardrobe: An actors clothing for a film or TV show.

Wardrobe Allowance: Payment to actors who use any of their pieces of clothing.

Wardrobe fitting: Once an actor is booked/hired they will be invited to try on the clothing the costume designer has chosen for them.

Weather Permitting: This is term used when during unplanned weather conditions a production can dismiss actors after 4 hours.

Wheelhouse: A person's area of expertise. A type of character or film/tv genre.

Wrap: Completion of filming a production, film, or television show/series.

Wrap Party: A celebration of the wrapping of a production and the culmination of everyone's hard work!

COMING SOON

In 2021 look for But, I'm Almost Famous?
An autobigraphical actor's journey!

Visit https://www.meganfordmiller.com for updates

ABOUT THE AUTHOR

Megan Ford-Miller

Megan with years of research, trial and error, self submissions, hundreds of hours of classes and a lot of determination helped her son Reid Miller get his first 18 IMDb credits and almost 30 jobs including commercial and print.

At 13 Reid had no acting experience, but he was driven and so was she. He has since had the great pleasure of working with people like Mark Wahlberg, Connie Britton, Alyssa Milano, Gary Sinise, Jenna Ortega, Maxwell Jenkins, Bill Paxton, Joe Mantegna, Frances Fisher, Monique Coleman, and the list goes on! They have worked together as a team and even after many years they continue to learn grow together as his career changes and evolves and they find new scenarios and challenges at every level.

@butimalmostfamous1 on Instagram & FACEBOOK
website- www.meganfordmiller.com

PRAISE FOR AUTHOR

"Classes teach you technique and you enter the business with desire and passion, but there's this window of time that occurs between your 1st audition and booking a job. Megan proves with expert guidance, you can actually shrink that window of time considerably."
>> Michelle K., Actor Parent

"It's easy to see this industry through rose colored glasses when you're new to the business and new to Los Angeles.
Megan's approach to sharing her knowledge with young actors is both positive and pragmatic.
She prepares the actor/actor's parent for the true expectations of the industry, which ultimately sets them up for a lasting career as an actor."
>> Abby J, Manager Los Angeles

"Working with Megan helped me tremendously! It definitely got me going in the right direction, otherwise I would have been walking around LA blindly."
>> Adam B, Actor

Made in the USA
Columbia, SC
25 January 2025